1042

©Text and illustrations by Andrea Wayne - von Königslöw, 1989

Peas, Please! was published in June, 1989, by Black Moss Press, 1939 Alsace Avenue,
Windsor, Ontario, Canada N8W 1M5.

Black Moss books are distributed in Canada and the United States by Firefly Books,
250 Sparks Avenue, Willowdale, Ontario, Canada M2H 2S4.
All orders should be directed there.

Black Moss Books are published with the assistance of the Canada Council
and the Ontario Arts Council.

This book was designed by Andrea Wayne - von Königslöw

Printed by the National Press, Toronto, Canada

ISBN 0-88753-191-1

To my family

Peas Please

Written and illustrated by Andrea Wayne - von Königslöw

Black Moss Press

Gilbert loved to play
with his food
right from the start.

Sometimes Mom and Dad
would play along.

As the years passed, he played more and more.

He had playing with food down to an art.

Children came from far and near just to see Gilbert
wear a pineapple hat, stick a bagel on his nose or juggle
Dad's meatballs and bounce them off his baby sister's head.

He charged them a nickel.

It soon became apparent that Gilbert
was playing more with his food than eating it.

This began to annoy his parents,
especially since he never ate his vegetables.

Peas were his favorite to play with.

"Eat them," said Mom.

"Throw them," said Gilbert.

He threw so many peas out the window
that the weatherman living below reported
that it was raining on a sunny day.

But things changed, as things do.

At the dinner table, Gilbert noticed that his peas were rolling around all by themselves.

The peas under his chair began to roll him away.

"Mom!" yelled Gilbert.

"Sit up, Gilbert," said Dad.

"But Dad...."

And they rolled him down, down,
to the place where matching socks,
missing buttons and old chewing gum go.

And when he got there,
the peas threw him high in the air.

They splashed ketchup on him,
put honey between his toes
and tickled him till he laughed so loud.

He was really having a wonderful adventure,
but soon he missed his Mommy.

"I want to go home now," Gilbert told the peas.

"No, we want you to stay and play," they said.

Gilbert felt a rumbling in his tummy
and an emptiness inside. He was just about
to cry when he remembered...

"I can eat you up!" he said to the peas.

And he stuffed his mouth so full that by the time
he had eaten them all, he looked like a balloon.

Up, up to the dinner table he floated.

Nobody had even noticed that he had gone.

"Look at the way Gilbert has eaten all his vegetables," Dad said to Mom.

"He must really love peas now," said Mom.

"We'll have them again tomorrow night."

"I'm eating at Benji's house tomorrow," said Gilbert.

He remembered that Benji is allergic to peas.